Terminally Poetic

Ouyang Yu

Terminally Poetic

Acknowledgements

Acknowledgements are due to the following publications, in which some of the poems in this book previously appeared:

New and Selected Poems (2004, Salt): 'can you write a bad poem', 'Going through the cards', 'A man of future speaks about love', 'The most unwanted man', 'Negative answers: an interview about poetry' and 'Terminally poetic'

Two Tongues, Two Hearts, and Rain-coloured Eyes (2002, Wild Peony Press): 'Making love, philosophically speaking'

The Eastern Slope Chronicle (2002, Brandl & Schlesinger): 'Silenced'

Atlanta Review (USA) (Spring/Summer 2002, p. 80): 'Theory'

ars poetica (No. 6, February 1998, p. 61): 'To all the poets i've read'

Gathering Force (No. 11, August 1997, p. 18): 'A word with the feminists'

LiNQ (Vol. 21, No. 2, 1994, p. 27): 'Untitled (b)' (living in oblivion)

Terminally Poetic
ISBN 978 1 76041 951 6
Copyright © text Ouyang Yu 2020
Cover photo: Ouyang Yu

First published 2020 by
GINNINDERRA PRESS
PO Box 3461 Port Adelaide 5015
www.ginninderrapress.com.au

Contents

A
About poetry — 10
Advice to a translator of Australian poetry — 11
An addition — 13
The agent's advice to an aspiring asian novelist — 14
Australia — 15
Australian — 16
Award — 17

B
Bad writing — 20
Big name — 21
The burglar — 23

C
can you write a bad poem — 26
Canadian memories — 28
A conversation — 32
Conversations with computer — 33

D
Displacement — 40

E
Economic censorship — 42
The editor's response — 43
An email message rejected — 44
Empty — 45
every second thousands of babies are born… — 46

F
Far and near — 48
For a change — 49

G
Going through the cards — 52

Guidelines for the American editors	53

H
How to write a worst seller	56

I
I am an intellectual	58
I did a word search	59
I don't want to write	60
I remember you said	62
I used to think	63
if I were to die	64
Illusions	65
Imagine	66
in a public place	67
Inquiry letter to a literary editor	68

J
Jealousy	70

L
Learn from Fiji: Australia!	72
Leaving things behind	73
Letter to the cross-cultural judging panel	74
Life of a poet	76

M
Making love, philosophically speaking	78
A man of future speaks about love	79
The meaning of China	80
Meeting poets	81
Memory/loss	86
A minimalist approach	88
Most editors	89
The most unwanted man	91
Moving	94
My poetry	96
My reader and i	97

N

Negative answers: an interview about poetry	100
No racism	102
Not communicating	103

P

The parachute	106
Pissing: a night scene	107
Placecommon	108
Poetry	109
A poet called today	110
The poet's obituary	112
The publisher's advice	113

Q

Quality	116

R

Reading poets	118
Reduced	123
Revision	124

S

The shame	126
Sick	127
Silenced	128
Snapshots of an awarding ceremony…	129
So to speak	131
Some editors	132
sometimes would you believe it	133
The stereotypical question	134
Statue of liberty	135

T

Talking with the famous writer	138
Temporarily untitled	141
Terminally poetic	144

The thing is	145
Theory	146
this is a pretty unhappy country	147
This is not a dream	148
This poem has been revised at least three times	149
This poem has not been revised	150
to a white/coloured editor	151
To all the poets i have read	152
to get an australian	153
To mankind	154
To the age of unreason	155
To think	156
To you in the bar	157

U

Untitled	160
Untitled (b)	161

V

Vision	164

W

Watching betty blue	168
What did they say when they read your poems	169
What is happening at this time of my life	170
What's wrong?	172
What title do you think this should be?	173
What went through my mind…t	174
Who's to blame?	175
why do we need to	176
Why do we so worry about the dates?	177
why do we write	178
A word with the feminists	180
World politics	181
Written at midnight	182
Written by one who doesn't know how to write poetry	183

A

About poetry

why should i write poetry at all when happy?
poetry is the sexual organ of pain
that becomes aroused at its bitterest
and ejaculates on contact of p and p

Advice to a translator of Australian poetry

you wanted me to make some recommendations to you as to
whose poetry in australia is
interesting enough to be translated into chinese?
i'm not sure whether you are more interested in the past or
the present
take the present okay?
there are big names of course
but you don't start with them or else you get stuck with them
start with small
things that have never been published
that are never allowed into print
oh yes what do you think australia is?
paradise? there is censorship believe me
about as bad as china and anywhere else
the only difference is they have a different name for it
they call it standards or quality
but you know what I call it?
I call it mediocrity whose name is australian poetry
avoid at any cost publications by major publishers
who don't know a thing about how to handle poetry except as
a marketing product
and whose main concern is the name
you still want the names?
you don't need me to tell you
they are there in every recent anthology
they are in the oxford companion of aust. lit.
or the cambridge hist. of aust. lit.
those who take up more pages than others
ask yourself these questions

why the others are never there
the Other that is
and if there ever is an anthology of unpublished australian poetry
a history of australian literary exclusions
and absences
why the worst still sits on top
and shits on others the Other that is
you still need the names?
i'm not a name dropper although i think i know a lot of them
save it for posterity
recommendations i don't have
not ever
and perhaps the only one i ever have is this:
find whatever that appeals to you at first sight
like love
and discard the rest
which is too much these days
bear in mind though
that poetry doesn't make money
even in a multimodern postcultural colonial post
2nd-class country
or go to a poet or critic at melb. uni.

An addition

to all the chinese stereotypes
i've studied –
there
are so many of them:
the one who steals small things
and white men's wives
the one who is miserly
turning one match box into ten
by thinly spreading the contents
the one who does dark things
in the dark
the one who easily gets frightened
with no heroic qualities
the one who keeps a placid face
of inscrewtability read inscrutability
the one who smiles oleaginously
the one who lies into truth
and the one who's aggressive
and likes to come here
of all the places
i just want to add this
stereotype of my own invention
who constantly acknowledges the legitimacy of those stereotypes
as being just like anybody else
except wrongly given the name chinese
and who can find a perfect match for that
in any australians

The agent's advice to an aspiring asian novelist

know that you are dealing with a white market
that demands to know three things about asia:
sex politics and exotic things
don't experiment even if you feel in your blood to do so
b traditional
b informative
b as pleasant as possible
and pleasing
the market is the thing
why make the publishers feel
that they are publishing you
to bankrupt
be always prepared to give in
to their tastes
that dictate
what you should write
and what you shouldn't
if you are still not sure
take a writing course
that i once took
and learn your trade
the easy way
by pay
as long as you can turn your words into coins
you are a dear
for this is a free democracy
where everything sells
if you can make it
but nothing is free

Australia

is a country for the old
the old on their verandas
like pieces of tattered clothes hung out to dry

australia watches
secretly
gleefully
its young die
of mental breakdown
in peace

Australian

I AM
proud of being
an australian

although
many of them
are not proud

of my being
an australian
you can easily

judge
by their i-wouldn't-care-less response
to my silly proud announcement

Award

i don't want it
you idiot
i am too old for such things

you never gave me
when i most desired it
and most deserved it

now you spite me
to honour me
as i am near my death

written
forty years or more
in anticipation

B

Bad writing

you reject me because i write badly
you reject me because i write ugly
you reject me because i write unintelligibly
you reject me because i write ungrammatically even ungraciously
you reject me because you are scared shit of my bad writing
because it turns your stomach
it stinks yes its stench right under your nose
i tend to agree with you
you are too good for me too fucking good for me
too bloody good for me
you and your bloody fucking good thing that you call arts
literature or poetry
that you write too good in english
i have been writing badly all these two hundred years don't
you know that
i have been using your fucking english to write badly don't
you know that
your english that is easy to fuck with but hard to use
your english that wins you prises but gives me shit
your english that excludes and extrudes us baddies
the 'bad chinese' remember the bulletin said a 100 years ago?
the bad chinglish that's me and my bad writing
written on your wall
and in your face

Big name

as my name is in the process
of being turned into a big name

sorry, i'll start again

i don't know why i am turned off
by the sight of big names

that litter page after page after page
of literary magazines

but i have my way of ignoring them
i simply skip them

skip them: robert adamson
les murray, kevin hart, blah, blah, blah

and i do the same to the big magazines
polished perfected quality shit

and i do the same to my own stuff
once it is published in them

i am sure no-one reads it
the proof is in the non-responding

i don't know if i can grab hold of someone on the street
and shout or whisper a line or two in his ears until he or she is moved

but i am sure
the police will come

and charge me
with indecent assault

that'll be good
for they will give me a chance

to record my poems
in the tape recorded interview

that the least-likely people: the police
the judge and the solicitors and barristers

will have to read
and listen to

The burglar

he steals everything
except poetry

C

can you write a bad poem

can you write a bad poem
like an ugly face
intentionally

a bad one that has no beautiful flowers or women in it
one that does not contain a nice metaphor
one that does not think of a nasty twist
one that does not evoke a reference to some great names or places
one that wants to keep cold or cool
a bit like just after you've had a good shit
one that does not want to claim to be a poem
one that turns every editor in the world off
because it simply doesn't work for them according to their personal
theories
or tastes
one that definitely doesn't contain sex because it wants to remain castrated for the moment
one that causes the ordinary people to make the comment that goes,
see, didn't i tell you that poetry has gone to the dogs these days!
and the critics to say:
this idiot can't even put his lines straight!
and the professors of english to say:
they should put english back on the agenda, no more cultural studies!
one that certainly can never win any prizes
because it says this to prizes of today:
fuck you all because you are exactly that: prizes of today
not of tomorrow
for tomorrow you die!

one that is so bad
that you feel this snot that i've just got out of my nostril with
the tip of my index
finger
and wipe on you

sometimes i really want to write bad poems
so bad that they can't be any good
as bad as me
as bad as this i
that keeps standing up
instead of remaining in the lower case

(let me check 'Change Case' under 'Format')

Canadian memories

it is all memory now. the mountains under the noon sun covered in hundreds of miles of snow glittering below the wings of air canada the only red maple leaf. the mountains beyond the border of america beyond human reaches glittering with metallic white. waves of mountains that roll me to canada a country where i dreamt once of going even as a lover of a gay the utmost punishment.

the night was singing much music at hotel vancouver. the guy with gappy teeth who sang nikita was such a consolation to me that the next day i had a photo of myself with fully exposed teeth and gums confident in its own ugliness. i couldn't get a wink of sleep that night what with the need for the shit which i should have relieved in the morning in china because of the jet lag what with couples of lovers making timeless love in bed on the lawn or anywhere they see fit under a t.v. made cloud. i tried to masturbate between the blanket and the white sheet but it was such a floppy disk that no words of energy could ejaculate onto the screen. early next morning i looked down my stories-high window to see an empty street lying so quiet that i wondered if i was really dead.

we went to a chinese restaurant called something like garden or whatever later i was to know that every chinese restaurant ended with a garden if not red light for on our way there our chinese friend carefully pointed out the semi-darkness dotted with female figures waiting for someone always waiting for someone near the chinese restaurant ending with the word garden. the place was called red light district my first sighted visual ecstasy.

tell you something about that. the ancient chinese word for a whorehouse is black building or green building which must be understood in its original transliteration *qing lou*.

then it was a long trip by car through the rocky mountains or the rocky trench as our manager told us. the arrow river with white waves curling so rapidly and banff like a big monument topped with sugar snow. the local bar full of people sitting on sticks talking in a strong accented english looking a bit shy.

we were going from toronto to niagara falls city. the driver had me beside him talking so fast about himself. streams of bright lights flying flashingly past on the other side. i asked what is the best and worst about canada having in mind of things connected with red light and stuff like that. ah well food is always good nothing really bad if you know what i mean but yea i know what you mean i was a drug addict you know i was so addicted that i was given up for lost it was god who saved me literally it was god now i had everything wife and children and a house everything. when we reached the place he gave me a package of *player* and i him one of *heng ta*. he lingered and i said *tip is it*? he winked and said well we'll see. the tall manager came back and i saw the driver approach him with a sign which is now like holding out his hand in a begging way but then only a sign. the manager just had a look at him not even scowling not even frowning just a look and the driver had to say good bye. i felt sorry for him ever afterwards and quite admired the manager for his skill.

and now it is montreal. the guy in the office said to me oh boy you should go to st laurent street. the girls there are so pretty so sexy particularly in summers. you should go. i had already been there despite the strict regulation that no one could go out unless in two or threes. the girls oh the girls the mere sight of them was a long wet dream. they stood on the streets so tall and naked that i could see the stars shining on their crutches and breasts. the black one was the night itself inviting one to enter her as soon as possible. the french girls leaning against the window of the bookshop were beckoning in french *vien vien ou bienvenue*. the mad question is still ringing in my ears how i managed to make love to them in french. a voice perched flying on the edge of my ear saying go out fifty dollars. blood flooded my senses and i was in a sexy swoon. all the street lamps looked like plump buttocks or bosoms and the street opened like a long deep vagina.

was that you browsing through glossy copies of fresh flesh mellow meat making a thousand plans to buy the strongest stuff and giving up at the last second and in the end offering your five blushed canadians for a *hustler* sitting bare bum on the sandy beach the bitch who made you such a chicken that you stole up the stairs like a thief with all the fucking couples in copulation squeezed between your chest and the sweaty shirt. and afterwards smearing them with seeds you have just brought in unchecked at the customs from an ancient but effete land.

but his is a different story. it is for later. always for later. until someone dies. to be written into a story. secure in a page. among words. he bought me a small bottle of maple sugar. how is it called my canadian editor do you know. in beds, two separate beds. we were telling each other dirty stories until we fell into sleep. he made me go hard against all the images of flesh and meat while remaining unperturbed. morbid, i told him. why morbid, he said, morbid means death. this is life. yes but you should go find a girl. i can't, i find them so soft like mud like rotten fruit like mushed potatoes like a piece of meat that i can't go in. well that is because you are so feminine. in his absence i looked out the window at the jagged skyscape lipsticked with neon and once more called a girl out from the page and fucked her dead.

canada oh cold canada. a memory that relates to michael tournier. to a long-distance call in a shanghai morning at a ramshackle telephone booth hearing a man telling me from another continent that he loved me feeling so funny. the two telegrams saying urgently call me collect at once this minute. my grandfather saying the foreign habit you know not caring spending a few easily earned dollars.

canada, i'm dead, canada

A conversation

the novelist says,

what are you?
a poet?
well, all you can do
is handle a few lines

the poet says,
you are not entirely right
in fact
i only handle one line

what is that?
says the novelist who makes millions of dollars in as many words

the line between life + death
the poet says

Conversations with computer

1

that's all right mate
i see my hands punching you thoughtfully
making mistakes here and there
i'm not waiting for anyone
only expecting something to happen
something is happening somewhere
someone must be dying at this moment
or being born
totally unrelated to myself
but i'm thinking of them or trying to
your noise nearly drives me mad
but i remain calm
i don't know who i am
what i am
what i want to do
how to do it if i do know
who cares
i'm in australia
who cares
you're a nice bloke though
you print everything i type into you
while remaining noisily silent
i can't bring myself to love you
but i have to use you
i have to speak to you compulsively
expecting someone to listen to it
in a faraway place
maybe a lot of people

a poetry reading even
where my words are happening
but who cares
they are all drinking
and laughing and
eating meat
and making love
and a lot of other things
poetry does not matter
conversation does
you tell me to go on with my nonsense
all right mate
two years ago
you wouldn't have thought me capable of such a feat
being in china
being in a place i didn't belong to
well you are right
i did not really belong anywhere did i
and i have never wanted to belong anywhere
so you said i was sort of flying
or to be more exact
i was sort of hanging in the air
floating
between heaven and earth
or is it between china and australia
who are they anyway
aren't they just two meaningless names
places which make you feel different

while you are really not
because
talking to you
i feel the night outside
never ever seeking to befriend me in the least
scratching my roof of head with branches of paranoia
and the lamp
of the slenderest body
in a standing position
that forever waits to serve
i know i am shit
i write shit
i can't be any good
having lost all my educated faith in anything good
including god
this my continuum of living
i write to sustain my sense of being
one with you
my sole companion at night
writing my life into you
becoming you
sowing my white seeds on your field of screen
even when i have nothing to say
my hands continue mechanically to grope
they want to live
that way

2

again, left without anyone to talk to
i come to you
with feeling fingers
what's the point of sitting before me without being able to come up
with anything to say
you wonder
what's the point of type/writing at all
when there's no one left in the world to read what you intend to write
except some faraway editors who don't really care
except me who register everything without a mind of my own
i'm very vulnerable you know
to any virus
of love and hatred
of any non-emotions as well
i'm easily lost
you'd better save me onto a hard dick
i mean a hard disk
but i don't have one
i let it be
gone with the sudden disappearance of electricity
the failure of the ubiquitous modern god
can you give me a bit of peace
i want to have a rest
from australians
who are so faraway
living their deathlike life?

3

sometimes i feel i could go on like this forever talking to you without feeling tired only feeling something akin to sadness emptiness self-pity deathliness of emotions all those things happening simultaneously without caring what i say what i do for i in fact do not say a thing only my hands my fingers are doing the typing instead of my tongue mouth lips it's an age of substitution things have lost their original meaning their original function take my mouth it does not utter a single word for days when it does it's a string of hot abuse or a chain of compliments so worn down with daily use and my hands tied up to a machine as a slave to serve its master the brain physical and electric without knowing whatever else they are good for it's something lamentable when everything dies god love literature poetry art except human beings the everlasting human beings and the machine

thus here face to face you and me the last remnants of the earth talking to each other in a onedimensional way you faithfully recording everything my fingers feed you and i whiling away my time filling all your 40 megabytes with my un/dying messages meant for the everlasting human beings

D

Displacement

reader has become the tyrant
god has become the customer

asians have become cauc asians
and caucasians have become american

celebrity has become the commodity
and commodities have become the adverts

politicians have become the prostitutes
and the prostitutes have become body engineers

greed has become a virtue
as both men and women want more

politics has become economics
as lawyers have become the mathematicians

the sky has become the largest billboard
and the air is up for sale

sex has become sexless
poetry has become a nonentity

and ultimately
the I has become a blue chip

E

Economic censorship

sometimes you'd think
political censorship is the worst form of human censorship
as when a chinese publisher rejects a book of mine
by saying that although this is a brilliant book in everything
we can't publish it because of the elements that will turn the stomach
of our leadership even if we know that you have got a grant
   to support it
and when all the other mainland chinese publishers echo the
   statement by saying
that is right we care less about money than about its political content
until you are sanctioned economically
as when a hong kong based chinese publisher says
we are happy to publish your book with all your financial support
and what's more
because hong kong is a small market for your book
you need to buy at least 1000 copies yourself
which we estimate to be worth between 10,000 and 20,000
   australian dollars
unless you pay
we won't be able to publish it

my decision is well-known
i mean to myself at least at this very moment
that i would rather cut my feet to fit their political shoes*
than rob a bank to fill their purse

---

* 'cutting the feet to fit the shoes', a Chinese idiom that means something similar to the 'Procrustean bed' or 'acting in a Procrustean manner'.

The editor's response

i suppose you can do whatever you like
you are certainly entitled to
it's a democracy where we live
but we do have our editorial policies
we maintain a high standard
so high only a few top writers can ever aspire to
decency propriety and an unshakable sense of social responsibility
and of course rationalism economic and always beauty
of language and of characters and of everything else along
canonical lines
if this is still not clear to you
you are welcome to purchase a few back issues of us
among our pages
we feature some of the greatest white australian writers
living or dead
never tinged with the slightest suggestion of an otherwise colour
in any case
we strongly recommend you to familiarise yourself with our style
and learn to write like them
your masters
by taking out a subscription
plus a 10%
gst

Erratum: I mean 'unshakeable' and 'moral' in line 7.

An email message rejected

'I'm sorry. I have tried everything possible but still can't send this message. I have given up. Following is your message kept intact. I haven't read it.' – internet company operator

Dear Z.Y.H.,
thanks for your info.
that no one's going to publish poetry
unless paid
i agree
poetry is a pain in the neck or the arse
but i still have to write it
i know no one's going to read it
but i still have to write it
i suppose i am sick
who is not?
never mind what they say
just do your thing
ok?

Empty

sending out poems to all over the world
and getting published
and read by unknown people
or perhaps by no one
as i am doing now
sending chinese poems to all over the chinese speaking world
and getting published
and read by unknown people
or perhaps by no one
and unpaid
until it is getting very late
and my back gets saw
and my eyes get tired
and my armpits get smelly
and my son and my wife get into bed

until you do not know what you are doing
why you are doing so
until

every second thousands of babies are born everywhere in the world

every second thousands of babies are born everywhere in the world
every second thousands of old people die their natural death everywhere in the world
every second men and women are making love and making hate
every second someone is writing a poem with his hand or in his head
every second that someone could be a she and could be an it
every second something is happening
every second i'm not necessarily thinking
every second we're drawing near i mean i'm drawing near something
every second death is closer
every second i've got someone somewhere waiting for my email messages
every second i just want to go to sleep
every second

F

Far and near

in australia
i am as far from any australians
as china is from australia

and i am as near them
as a cloud
near the sky

For a change

how is a man going to change himself in his late 30s
i happened to think of this
when i was washing my feet
a little past midnight
when no longer anything was happening
except the regular on and off of
a loyal refrigerator devoted entirely to ice

vaguely i remembered a dream i had had some time ago
about the age-problem and how to cope with it
was it i who faced it or someone else
or both

i've seen people who tried it
jumping from body to body
living a life of infinite penetrabilities
supposedly

i've seen women dressed so young
that they looked more fuckable than marriageable
except that they gave a face that had the surface of a hard nut
when they turned around to peer at you

i have
thought of many changes:
change of my blood
change of my body
change of my yellow skin
and a bracing of my abnormal teeth

even now as i'm gazing at myself in the mirror
of ephemerality
at my own hallowed image as a barbarian god
i feel bored
how can a man suffer a life that is worshipped
with only worship
and see a sky printed all over in capital letters
with his name only

in one's late thirties
one feels the need for a change
so one goes outside and suddenly becomes aware
that the newly mowed lawn of the neighbour's
is silent with the falling darkness
while in one's own rank garden
neglected for weeks
totally abandoned to laziness
crickets become so loud with their songs
for the approaching autumn
that one is left wondering
why he should be bothered at all

G

Going through the cards

sometimes they give you the idea that australia is some pure
land called *terra australia incognita* or *australa felix* stuff like
that or they let you think that australia is called cook or
murray or white or uk or robinson or howard or dyson or
morgan or nolan or jennings or gould or hughes or carey or
martin or hanson or woodard or american or

going through the cards that kind of australia is dissolved in
names like arranga or zareski or chan or ng or pitruzzello or
karogiannis or truong or wang or zhang or ouyang or xiao or
strangio or asuncion or plousi or petrovic or abdulatiff or
kovacevic or de jong or ubaldi or van leeuwen or choy or lista
or banitsiotis or teoh or wong or kee or da costa or quattrone
or moulin or marafioti or mudrooroo or oodgeroo or ginibi
or huang

still all you get to hear when you are put on hold or being put
through is this helen or margaret or dick or david or doug or
dicky or sam or ian or merv or geoff or peter or simon or les
or john or richard or judith or judy or justine or jane or jo or
joe or junk or jeff or tom or terry or tony or tongue or tealby
or ross or rose or ronnie or roy or ron or rot or raunchy or
rainy or ray or ring or james or bill or bob or bunny or kim
or king or yvonne or

makes you wonder what this identity business really is and if
a yellow pages is more australian than any genuine
anthologies of literature and poetry put together can ever be
and if all these bunches of business cards i've spent years
collecting in australia – and there are not many years: only 9
– are not a real australia: realer than either you and me

Guidelines for the American editors

• in an electronic age you are advised that you should look at electronic submissions to save time or else suffer the loss of good contributors
• i'm currently not sending you anything unless you are really worthy of something but if you are i won't send you anything unless you ask for it or unless i'm in a mood for it or unless you change that hypocritical policy of having a website promoting your magazine but opposing valuable electronic submissions
• you're advised to remove the submission guidelines unless you put this *Guidelines for Editors* side by side to it because it is certainly not democratic to have only the guidelines for contributors not for editors
• you are not allowed to insist on international authors including a reply coupon because it is not economically viable for them and if you don't understand this become one yourself
• you may accept or reject anything i send you without ever bothering to return it for i don't want you to return it at your own expense if you know what i mean therefore no postage will ever be included for your privilege
• if you don't even read unsolicited manuscripts authors send you at their own expensive expense the authors will never read your magazines simple as that
• what am i looking for? i'm looking for editors who don't pretend to be some gods sitting there passing judgements and making out as if they were the gatekeepers and authors were beggars trying to get in
• you may make your enquiries to me at <youyang@bigpond.net.au> if you are looking for something new
• contribution time averages a life
• previously published work is not acceptable unless it is bad

• think twice if you don't understand this
• multiple not to say simultaneous submissions are definitely acceptable these days (think of webporn that is being watched)
• upon acceptance of my work you will receive a complimentary copy of my other contributions
Thank you for reading this guideline and bear in mind that in this age of equality if you reject me i'll reject you!

H

How to write a worst seller

is prompted by the title of an article once published in the melbourne *age*
I can tell you this write away

rule 1 right in a way no editors like
rule 2 rite only for the tiny and tiny publishers and if need be
self-publish it

rule 3 wright with no rules and regulations in mind as if nothing
had been written before
rule 4 write and be happy with the thought that only one person
in the world will read it

half of that is yourself
and the other half: yourself too

I

I am an intellectual

i sell my mind
like they do
their bodies

for cheaper rates

i don't care about nationalities
i pick up their language
because it sells

like hot whores

be they imperialists communists postcolonialists
or feminists
i work for them

as long as they pay in money and name

i like to change isms
like a man or woman his or her underwear
for something more sexy

and progressive

i have no other principle
than you pay me and i serve you
my mind is a machine

educated for the purpose

i am an intellectual for you
who are willing
to book me early

I did a word search

i did a word search
for ass
in my elegant essay
designed for an elegant journal
for an elegant sum of money
because i did not want any ass inserted between the lines
my loyal computer
did a thorough search
picking up:

associated with the powerful
passionate lovers
classic music
and even essay as a possible deviation:

essay: suggested correction: assay?

I don't want to write

but i have to
you know what i mean?

i've packed four boxes
of magazines and newspapers, all literary, today

that contain my published stuff
from all over the chinese and english speaking world

it makes me sad
to think of the waste

as I was packing them
the thought came to me

that this was probably the last time
i'd do this

it actually felt like that
clearing out a life literarily lived

wondering as i often do these days
that if I had another life after this

i would be most likely to do other things
a businessman for example or simply a good for nothing

sometimes you'd think poetry is like shit
once stuck in it you'd never wash it clean like the yellow river

i've observed a few people
who never touch poetry

doctors for example
stockbrokers and plumbers

but this has nothing to do with that
this, if anything, has to do with

the poetry that i don't want to write
but i've been righting all my life

it's a wrong enough life
that only ignorant future generations can glorify

or condemn
if i had another life

god, i'd do anything but this

I remember you said

girls
everywhere

are
shallow

they
are

deep
only

when
men

enter
them

it's a
poem

i
said

I used to think

westerners including australians are better
more honest
more brainy
more body
and etc

i now wonder
than whom?
than themselves?

if I were to die

if i were to die
and be reborn
the voice says to me
i wouldn't be a poet again
there are so many more interesting things
in the world
i mean so many more
that you wouldn't even know
what to choose

guess what i'd respond to that

i don't know yet
let's give death a go
and see

Illusions

before they disappear
i'd better confine them within my lines
it's true that
every time when
i hold the mobile phone
to my ears
I expect that
it explodes against my brain
when the machine appears in my window
flying overhead
i thought it may be crashlanding on
my roof
when someone rings up
my receiver may turn into
an electrical gun
when i hold my penis in
my hand pissing
it may break from its root
when

Imagine

how boring it would be
if this world was turned into a literary one

littery people babbling about
the bestseller lists awards festivals and what have you

i would prefer it
as it is

like in a court
with all the potential criminals

to whose stories i would be kept busy listening
better than anything literary

in a public place

in a public place
such as a restaurant
people take notice of you
only when you behave badly
like farting loudly
or blowing your nose loudly
into a tissue
(sometimes people even get used to this)
or putting your index finger into your nostrils
one by one
then flipping it out with your thumb
or talking dirty
or laughing uncontrollably
or only to yourself while alone
but no one takes notice of you
when you don't do any of these things
even if you are probably a very famous poet
in a private place
leaving you to yourself
reading a book or a mind

Inquiry letter to a literary editor

what sort of stuff would you like
mild or wild or child
mad or sad or just bad or simply sallad or ballad
does anything go
if not
does nothing do
or anything you like goes
what standard is that:
i like therefore you like and they all like
sorry i should confine myself to inquiries
do you publish non-poetry as in non-fiction
or non-drama or non-literary stuff
do you i hope this is not offending you
publish what no one has written about
not even shakespeare
and all the literary winners of nobel-prizes
that i have written
and you can't judge
by any standards
what if all this is just pure
non-poetry
what if
i attempt to
unwrite

J

Jealousy

the other thing is
as soon as someone announces that the book he's going to read
has won a prize
i lose interest
i'm such a self-lover
that I only like someone
who loves my own work

L

Learn from Fiji: Australia!

– à la George Speight

when you find it hard to get rid of your top guy
howard what's his name

when you can't even get him to say a simple sorry
mate i mean mates

when you still have got a couple of years
before you can vote him out

when you have to put up with all that shit
gst – get shit to eat, is it?

learn from fiji
i mean follow me

stage a coup
and stick it up his arse

whoever it is
don't brag to me about democracy

if you can't even cure the disease
that it breeds

take up your guns mates
that he has melted into money

do something: stage a coup
or be his duck soup

Leaving things behind

as i drive down the information superhighway
i leave everything behind
the twentieth century

with its drive towards
today
and my 44 years

i leave things behind
mountain-high years
that i'd need a telescope to reach

i leave things behind
my empty mind
bent on progress

i leave things behind
my day by day dreams
erased by living practice

i leave things behind
that i once treasured
and no longer value

i leave so many of my selves behind
to arrive
at me

i leave things
behind
even as i write this

Letter to the cross-cultural judging panel

subject yourselves to the selection criteria
before you subject me to it

let me ask you how many of your have a second language
and don't evade the question by answering you have a second marriage

you impose in your sel.cri. all conditions ESSENTIAL or HIGHLY DESIRABLE
my only trouble with it is they all mean the same thing to me as:

white faces are ESSENTIAL or HIGHLY DESIRABLE
or else why does my face turn your hearts cold as soon as you see it?

it's now two thousand and one
but another year of your successful effort in barring another face of your colonisee

from your university that welcomes asian money
and keeps out asian minds

yes i know you've just recruited another malaysian or singaporean
or hong kongese or sri lankan or indian or fijian or

brethrens of your commonwealth who speak your lingo
with an imitation accent that you feel comfortable with

and i know, mr white, what is going through your mind
as you flip through my application

we'll never allow this person to come in
he's simply too bloody good for us

what if he rocks the boat?
what if he takes possession of my professorship?

what if he challenges the vice-chancellor's position
we must make sure our democracy remain intact

from such aggressive intellowctuals
no matter how good they are

even if a mixed country now and god save us
we must keep our hearts snow-white and clean

which is the least we can do
with the exchange of just a glance and a whisper

we keep things under control
mate, this 'is the best bloody country in the world

and i am sorry for any poor bastard who doesn't live here'
and no apology for anyone like you who do live here but never make it

and never will

Life of a poet

you spend the first half of your life
turning yourself into a collection

and the next half
giving it away for free

M

Making love, philosophically speaking

is a boring thing
no poetical metaphors are forthcoming
body is the message

gazing into each other's eyes
sees other images
inside one is inside many

the near becomes the distant
the mind a balloon
floating some sky else

reaching climax
like reaching everest
down is death

post making love
is an age
when one sleeps

A man of future speaks about love

i mean why do you have to bother
the japanese have practised surgically removing their appendix
at an early age longer than any culture in the world
so do we
get rid of the instinct for love at one remove
by using hi-tech instruments
the human body is nothing
but an index to the mind
an index that contains all kinds of cross-references
as many times as you would like to cross
we now produce babies by the tube-loads
or put them away by euthanasia
love?
i have never heard that word being said
nor seen it being used
they'd be laughing their heads off to hear me say it
although i know
that they did use it
as a kind of aphrodisiac
when they have sex
to make the whole thing feel nice

oh yes
there are some scholars
specialised in love
as an ancient tradition
that is going out of fashion near the end of the twentieth century

The meaning of China

everything changes
there
i said
to alex
over the mobile phone
in my car
this afternoon
on my way
to the county court
except one thing
what is it
he said
the chinese flesh
oh, he said
it is the oldest thing
that remains fresh
unchanged
despite change
that turns china
west
oh
he said again
look at me
i said
the chinese skin
wrapping up
an australian heart
and
look at you
an english skin
wrapping up a chinese
'art

Meeting poets

didn't meet a poet myself until i was well over twenty or thirty can't remember
but did meet lots of people who wrote poetry
lots of queer people who became even queerer when they started writing poetry
one in particular who pennamed himself Blue Peace
drifted momentarily to me
he was so handsome that he said he could seduce any girl who happened
to cross his path with his eyes fixed on her
however his love tactics just would not work on a girl he called Big Teeth who never seemed to like him one inch
when he left the school i told him that he would not be writing any more poetry in ten years
my prophet eye having already seen the death of the young poet in him
he was not happy and did not give me anything back in return for the book of poems i gave him as a gift
or perhaps he was being a poet not tied to secular formalities?

the other guy who wrote poetry was one who could not even properly write a well-constructed
chinese sentence and all his poems that he showed me
were simply strung together by a sense of nonsense
however when he started reading his poems accompanied by quite unrelated music
from the tape recorder i was so strangely moved
that i went away thinking that it should not be like that
five years later when i saw him again he talked to me excitedly about an academic career
teaching english as second language
his name was Any Smooth

the real poets who published highly visible names i never met
except on photos or tv
i mean the chinese ones
i did have the luck of meeting a poet unheard of in china but
much talked about overseas
because of his unheardofness
likewise i was unheard of by him as a poet
the curious desire of letting the real poet see an unreal poet in me
was aroused
i showed him four sheets of paper onto which i copied some
of my early stuff
in clear and serious schoolboy hand
he read them page by page
put them back in order
drank the beer i bought for him
did not say a word
(i was saying for him:
what did this guy want me to do?
to say it's good to please him?
or to say it's bad to offend him?
i'd better keep my poet's gold mouth shut
the best way to deal with such aspiring ones)
said something like:
the weather in melbourne is strange
rain one moment and sunshine the next
the only feeling i had then was an instant vow that i'd never
show any of my stuff to a poet
particularly a real and famous one

it's all coming back now
i did meet some chinese poets in my life
i think when i was over thirty maybe thirty-two or
thirty-three
when a meeting was arranged between an australian poet and
a bunch of shanghai poets
at ecnu
all the other poets were so childish chirping like sparrows
about the beauty of their home
counties that the australian poet, rather relieved
started talking about some new trend in australian poetry in
making poems like cutting
pictures immediately from tv or making them exactly like
what appears on a tv
only one poet made any impression by the way in which he
looked at the people without
making any comment
he was Palace Seal
whose poems i read and found interesting to a degree
i thought i identified with him
so i sent some poems to him
in reply he sent a book of poems of his to me
again without making a single comment on my poems
you know what i did to his shit?
i never read one poem of his

on the contrary real and famous poets (what does that mean really?)
were quite forthcoming with their poems or books of poems
even when you did not ask for it
i found them tiresome
one in particular from melbourne whose name i'd refrain
from mentioning
because i did not want to hurt feelings
gave me a book of his published things
and set about tidying his desk while saying 'well, i guess it's
about time
i did some work' thus dismissing me in a rather unpoetical way
like a shrewd businessman hoping that some day one line or two
might find their way to obscure chinese hands through my
translation
did i mention translation of his poems not accepted by anybody
i did but i did not say i wrote poetry
well done mate someone said to me over my shoulder
i turned round and saw the shadow of my matured and
cynical youth
cast across the length of the island continent
i have learnt

as for other poets
they were just too much on the wrong side of life
i tried my best to avoid them
if they told me to wait for their car to come and pick me up
at three-thirty i'd believe them but
say goodbye and get going convinced that somehow that car
would break down halfway

or if they invited me to a party i'd check the address twice
before i started my engine and
would still find myself in a place that had more than a dozen
of exactly the same names
or if i was told that i was meeting one of the best australian poets
she or he turned out to be someone entirely unimpressive
and boring
courteous maybe
but boring

let me not meet any more poets
designed for pleasures of poverty
and perversity
let me finish with them once and for all
and live a life free from
poetry of troubles

i think i can already hear their protests

Memory/loss

sometimes
memory
like a key
gets lost
temporarily
but now
it gets lost
like a title
it does
the title
of my book
my book of chinese
poetry
in which
i write things
like serial poetry killer
or serial poet killer
and fake things like
china
for some reason
i just can't recall it
although i do remember
sending it to a friend based in london
who said he was a lover
of high modernism
and that he was not abhorred
but rather puzzled by the book
and i think
that has started it all
by now

my mind
remains barren and blank
the title gone
from memory
although I only finished the book
slightly less than
a month
ago

i do remember though
he gave it to a phd guy
he supervises
and i'd love to see
what he says in his phd

A minimalist approach

what is life?

making friends?
making love?
making money?

and what else?

well
making death
liveable?

Most editors

most editors
are stupid

you say

they wait
for big names

forever putting
small potatoes aside

i cheated them
you say

by changing my name
from big to small

they trash it
not able to tell a pearl

from the eyeball of a fish
they want to look good

sometimes shit
looks pretty pretty

you say
and only stinks

years later
in certain cases

pages later
but the stupid editors

get paid
their chosen fish

get paid
for their opaque eyeballs

and you
you say

remain as small
as an

o

The most unwanted man

he moves among the books
glancing from cover to cover the way he is used to doing
from fruit stand to vegetable when he goes to the market
or when he goes to a jewellery shop
where he wonders why he's there
the names the titles the photos
of the famous and infamous people
he kept his lips tight shut
and thought there was someone behind him watching
turning around he saw rows and rows of printed images
staring at him
in dumb accusation:

why are you here?
got anything to buy?
if not why here at all?

he felt for the fifty-dollar note in his pocket
and told himself that he would not buy anything
he did not know why
only vaguely that he would never buy anything that did not contain
his own writing
selfish yes
narcissistic yes
but the paradox is that he never wrote anything
how could he buy his own writing
he laughed inwardly at this absurdity
of regarding something being written as having been already published

something like the title of this poem
The Most Unwanted Man
a novel that he has seen published by Penguin or Angus & Robertson
or Faber and Faber or whatever that claims to be a good publisher
featuring the total view of a back turned upon the world
a multiple back that contains the man's childhood adulthood
and old age
in the shape of inner rings of a cut tree
the book begins with something like this:

i can't understand why i was born but suppose i had to be
born after all
because it was by pure coincidence that they had me

the words reminded me of the lines i was composing
yesterday on my way
back from the uni when i thought how accidental my life was
inhabiting a body that was borrowed from some/bodies else
that when i surprised upon them those listless strangers
waiting for their
buses home how much like a chance i must have looked to them

but let's get back or go on
did it come out of an interior rejection of things at large
a denial of everything unattached to you
and something alien in yourself

he is now quite aware of the change of tone and the points of view
in the branching of the poem
and diagnoses that as
a bewilderment of not knowing what to do
with himself yourself myself
for being unwanted

Moving

you would have thought there's nothing moving these days
but let me tell you these two anecdotes or true mini-stories
there's a poet in china whom i've never met before
and he contributes to my magazine regularly
with his poetry in which I remember one thing he says
'pornography is a healthy word'
although i've been unable to choose any of his poems, i don't think
but i've chosen poems from the ones he has recommended
by virtually unknown poets in china
each time he sends their work
he tells me in his letter
he has to copy the poems one by one onto a piece of paper in
his neat hand
so that I can read them
this is not a single page or a single poem
there is page after page of poetry
copied in long hand
there's another poet in china whom i've published in my magazine
and who recently emailed me a poem that i've chosen of
another poet in china
he told me that because that poet whose poem i've accepted
had no access to a computer
or any email facilities
he had to read out his poem word by word over the long
distance telephone

for this poet to input in his computer and email to me
now in this competitive world of ours where ceos, doctors
and lawyers
have no time even to shit
these are the things that, curiously, move me

Recorded on my way after visiting the biannual melbourne arts show called *Melbourne Artfare 2000* held in the Royal Melbourne Exhibition Hall on 8 October 2000, Sunday, at 5.50 in the afternoon, sunny afternoon, with shadows of the trees lying across the road; yellow wattle flowers every once in a while.

My poetry

has turned sour
from bad to worse
i don't know how to write poetry
whenever i think of prizes that lie ahead of me
and of the famous ones that are certain to win them
i become tedious
i find poetry irrelevant
as i said to a friend over the phone this afternoon
in chinese
using a chinese proverb:
poets are 'broken pots that break themselves brokenly'
meaning what?
meaning that since they are broken
they can afford to break themselves more
making the noise with the ever diminishing pieces
i look at my poetry
it certainly looks like broken pieces
that do not even make a noise
i write
with a sense of ever growing futility
and failure
like the life itself
as it seconds towards
death
my poetry

My reader and i

like two strangers
sitting
in a tram

facing
without looking at
each other

and departing
at different times
and venues

N

Negative answers: an interview about poetry

q. do you read any australian poetry?
a. no. not really. why?

q. what about those big ones such as les murray and peter porter?
a. isn't peter porter a british guy? no. i didn't read him.

q. and murray?
a. you mean les murray? isn't that the sbs hungarian guy who
              comments on succor – sorry, how do you spell it?

q. soccer, i think.
a. oh, he writes poetry, does he? about soccer games?

q. skip this (muttering to himself). you know who's winning what?
a. what's winning who? what you mean?

q. you yourself a poet?
a. no. i'm not. why would I?

q. didn't you used to get published a lot under the name of
                        youyangs or something?
a. you mean the youyangs? or ouyen? no. i never did, actually.
                          it's the aboriginal words.

q. you know some poetry anthologies published recently?
a. no, like what?

q. like john leonard's oxford anthology.
a. oh, no. i didn't. leonard da vinci. isn't that the great italian
   painter? how come he edited australian poetry? and oxford?
            so, was it published by the english? in england?

q. i suppose so. i don't really see the difference. anyway. let's
            go on. you know it is available in big bookshops.
a. oh is it really? so what? who gives the fuck? i don't.

q. and john tranter and philip mead's penguin book of
            australian poetry?
a. no. is mead margaret's brother also specialising in anthropology?

q. oh my god (muttering to himself again). but did you ever go
            buy such books?
a. rubbish! why? why would i buy such things?

q. why not?
a. i don't know. don't ask me.

q. is that because they don't include any asians?
a. probably – but what has that got to do with me. i'm not asian.

q. but you look like one.
a. do i? fuck it, do i? you look more like one than me because
            you wear characters on your chest.

q. that's getting confusing. you've got a comfortable life in
            australia, don't you?
a. me? materially or spiritually or culturally or sexually or whateverly?

q. whateverly then, if you prefer that way.
a. fuck, i don't know. don't ask me these stupid questions. let me
            down this beer.

q. all right. can i join you?
a. oh yeh, why not? no worries. i'll shout you.

No racism

if you're a cathy
free

man

or
an alan

duff
or
a yoyo

ma
or
a sumi

jo
or
a vane
ssa
mae
or
a michael
ondaa
tje
there's no such a thing
as rac
is
m
if you know what I mea
n
if you are a fujimor
i

Not communicating

the editor
who hates him
never gives him a chance
until he dies

and he
unaware of it
keeps sending in his stuff
until he dies, too

his last remark
as his first
remains the same:

no need to return the rejection
use the back for whatever purposes

P

The parachute

this is not a dream
but when he walks into it
he feels like in one
for he refuses to even sit in the business class
of a 777
on a free trip to america
he refuses to go anywhere by air
he prefers the slowness of land and water
unless
he says
he's equipped with an automatic
parachute
that will launch him
into somewhere alive
in the event of a multiple death

Pissing: a night scene

in the unconscious hours of the night
i got up from a long dream of dreaming of toilets
to relieve myself
and being turned away by the closed doors or crowds of pissers

i went to the real toilet located at the furthest end of the house
and was surprised to see the kitchen lit up
in a flood of moonlight streaming in from the gossamer lace

turning away from that i saw through the side window
street-lamps in the distance
ripe with orange colour
heavy with night dew
as if to beckon me to eat them

shiveringly
i pissed and went back to bed
wondering about life without toilets

Placecommon

i was reading this buddhist book
much of it is common place
too much of it is place common
but probably nothing is more
commonplace or placecommon
than this where it says, in chinese:
zhi ren zhi shi chang
which translates into english as:
a perfect person is only an ordinary person
it's not commonplace i know
nor placecommon
but i like it

Poetry

he never has to have it in his life
never wants to
finds it too sentimental
not worth the time and energy
basically
he doesn't want to have anything to do with it
silly
even babish
he hasn't spent a cent
on a single line
and he's happy about it
he'd clone his fortune
his wife's beauty
his son's intelligence
and his daughter's youth
in fact
he'd clone anything worth something

except poetry

A poet called today

i was reading my own stuff
checking my spelling
by the kitchen table with a french window nearby that
received full sunlight
as i said to my wife the other day
my study should really be located in the kitchen
not where it was facing a prison wall with wiring outside the window
that separated us from our neighbour
when my phone rang
and the stranger's voice revealed a poet's name
in fact
a famous poet's name
who invited me to attend his book launch
and said that this was a personal invitation
i was delighted
we exchanged some greetings
things like: how are you?
are you busy writing?
things like that
things that probably writers ask when they ring each other
i don't know
because few writers ring me these days
nor do i ring anybody
because a poet personally invited me
i thought i must personally go
but should i buy the book?
i mean should i
if not, would i offend?
what is the politics in all this?
who should i go to and consult with?

when I thought of what i had told him what i had done
it was near 10 at night
i said I had been writing chinese poetry and the poems i had written
could cram into three or four books
i meant that for a joke
but there was no return joke coming or forthcoming
i felt a bit put out
so what's the politics in all this?
i thought i should have asked him then and there
perhaps i should not have told you this
because i did not mean to boast or anything
but now it was 14 past 10
at night

The poet's obituary

others have commented on his poetics
i have not
even read a single line
all i can remember
is that
the guy has always been sitting
there
in the semi-darkness
of his own shadows
among the audience of my reading
wearing a perennial hat
that suggests baldness
underneath
the guy has never said
a single word in his life
to me
until after his death
when i have to say this
myself

The publisher's advice

anything that sells
goes

although
not the other way round

we do publish trash
only because it's smash

and s/hit
too

and it
goes

Q

Quality

there is nothing in his life
that matters more than
quality

as he often says:
quality is my second life

until one day
he dies a
quality death

as you can see
death is only secondary
to his second life

R

Reading poets

1

the ancient chinese poets are not read but recited
somehow they are all sad
tens of thousands of years sad:

yanpo jiangshang shi ren chou
one is made sad on the misty wavy river

choudao duanshui shuigenliu jubei jiaochou chougenchou
the water flows more the more you cut it with your sword
and the heart becomes sadder the more liquor you pour on it

erjin shijing chouziwei yusuo huanxiu yusuo huanxiu
now that i've had my fill of sadness i'd say no more say no
more about it

jianbuduan lihuanluan shilichou bieshi yifan zhiwei zaixintou
the entanglement of sadness cannot be cut loose with scissors
and refuses to be sorted out

wenjun nengyou jiduochou qiashi yijiang chunshui xiangdongliu
can i ask how sad you are oh i am as sad as a riverful of spring water
that flows eastward

*baifa sanqianzhang lichou shigechang buzhi mingjingli hechude
qiushuang*
my white hair is three thousand *zhang** long
my sadness as long as myself

when i see the autumn frost in the mirror
i wonder where i get it

i don't read those sad chinese poets any more
they sadden me with their useless poems
i wonder if they could understand the sort of feeling i am having now
if they lived here like me do
having to turn a hard-worked imagination into reality
in a space that's least of all human
having to live
like i have never lived before
with objects objects objects

2

the english poets are not recited but read
the first ones that started me were found in the golden treasury
it was a laborious affair
copying the long and short poems that i liked into my
exercise books
– three thick ones of them –
below the fluorescent light in the university dormitory
when everybody was doing their homework
i didn't really understand the ancient lines of those small islands
but i persisted reading from beginning to end
line by line stanza by stanza
while my thoughts were somewhere else
my ears were receiving the loudest calls of frogs in the night
ponds outside
to each other
my nose smelling the scents of the chinese scholartrees
myself fallen into a dreamy reverie
it was like drinking a glass of foreign wine that you neither
knew the name

or quality of
but each drop
like each word
affected you as if it carried within itself something magical
that defied understanding and at the same time deepened the intuitive
perception
your taste bud blossomed overnight
the copywriting act in itself was like a copying of my own accompanying
thoughts
and a writing of my own hidden poetry

those innocent carefree days were succeeded by more troubled poets
such as wilfred owen
whose lines drew me to his black tunnel where he met death
or the stone on which the soldier's kiss was redder than their blood
or sylvia plath
with her monomaniac relations with her father
her dream-like madness so beserk that i stopped reading her
fearing that something similar within me might break out one day
or ted hughes
who introduced horses crows and other animals
in a quiet scholarly way
but with a power that leaves the mind going back again and again

3

the american poets are neither read or recited
there are too many of them
some are so casual
like robert frost whose lines about the wall
or the divided roads are as plain as them
and as there
some like walt whitman
create an ocean-like monotony
emily dickinson the recluse
feeds an army of good-for-nothing-else academics
it is the small ones i like best:
robert mazey
whose prowling fearfully at night near the house of a naked woman
sleeping beside the open window
mark strand
whose dogs eating books barking with possession
whose husband and wife
blown apart by the polarised winds
and then there is edgar lee masters
with his small monuments of words
to ordinary beings like me
that make you wonder
if one day you would not like to write something like that
for yourself

american poets
there are so many of them

4

australian poets
australian poets?
skip them over
i am not one of them

5

french poets well french poets
are really something
baudelaire who nearly made me vomit reading him
appolinaire whose grave on the beach type of thing
is monotonous enough
and groups after groups of poets
who like to give themselves airs and names
such as surrealists etc etc
while german poets like goether
and heine
are a constant enjoyment to read
in chinese translation

but who can remember them
except their names?

* a Chinese unit of measurement about three and a third metres.

Reduced

this is a status-reduced people
who live a reduced level of language
in a reduced position
at a reduced living standard and price
with reduced self-respect
reduced self-expectation
and reduced self
but
first, and last, of all
they seem happy
with the reduction
and it's not for me
to take pity

i don't even want to know them

Revision

they talk about it as if it were their god
REVISION
they talk about it with reverence
they say,
>i revise this 99 times or I write this novel for 10 years
>i could have taken 100 years to write it life permitting

i hear them say behind or below that:
>i am just great because I can revise every word of mine till it is perfect

do i believe that?

Capitalism now dictates that the human mind be a machine that must revise it
to perfection to reap maximum profits
against the human nature that tends to grow like wild grass
which, no matter how ugly, never shows any desire to revise itself
nor do the clouds in the sky which are so imperfectly perfect
or perfectly imperfect that they change
instead of revise
when it comes to poetry
same thing: a cloud to the mindsky

S

The shame

always
when you do something
even when you think of something

you wonder if it is right
according to *their* standards
or whether *they'll* not find you mercenary-minded

often
you simply give up on anything
when you meet face to face with it

that you once thought is your better half

Sick

he gets this feeling
when he reads his own poetry
published along with others
after the magazine arrives
or when there is no response
for years
to his meaningless endeavour

he gets sick
when he finally realises
that life is perhaps
not unlike death
in its solitary condition
confinement
the only difference being
you hang up
on the former
while the latter hangs up
on you
no communications there
either way

he is getting sick
but he won't mention it
for diversion
he picks his teeth
with an unbent clip

Silenced

the voice
when silenced
creeps out of fingers

the words
when silenced
constipate

the trees
when silenced
expatriate

the heart
when silenced
transplants

Snapshots of an awarding ceremony: slightly out of sequence

a.

i said didn't see any writers he said you wouldn't perhaps because they were hiding themselves at home writing I said well if they were not shortlisted they wouldn't turn up he said that's right

b.

i saw a man in his seventies getting his poetry prize a white man i saw a man in his late fifties getting his fiction prize a white man I saw a lot of white-skinned white-haired men and women around me peppered by brown people and yellow people who were the only ones sitting the weak ones

c.

a man read or rather recited from a play and ended his performance with a loud FUCK that caused everyone to applaud and shout and shriek with laugher in the presence of premier and arts minister a female the white woman behind me didn't seem to be very pleased but she didn't say anything

d.

a woman an old one asked are you vietnamese i said guess again she said you look like a vietnamese that i once taught in adult migrant education centre i said guess again i mean give it another go she said ah well i can't i said china chinese you know she said oh does that make any difference i said

e.

she asked when i got home why you came back so early is
that because no-one paid any attention to you again i said no
she said yes it must be like last time or every time but i said
no i had fun thinking of my weariness my urge to say fuck
my instinct about people i dislike my reluctance to go and
congratulate anyone who's won a prize even the one i've
judged to be the winner my wonderment why big names
keep winning prizes why they make themselves so lonely and
why so few people go to them to say nice things why they pat
each other on their backs to congratulate themselves why
people feel so important after they win but not before what
makes a human being a full human being not a less or more
one as i trudged towards my car somewhere near a city public
bathhouse

So to speak

when someone wrote some very good stuff
my father would
instead of saying how beautiful the writing is
say,

this bastard
or the dog-fucker

his mother's cunt
how bloody well he writes!

but of course
that's dirty chinese
that refuses to translate into
decent english

for decent english ears

Some editors

it seems
have been rejecting people
all their life

there's such hatred in them
for their own inability
to discover themselves

while others
have spent all their life
promoting their likes

fortunately
i'm lucky to read
the rejected work

of
charles
bukowski

sometimes would you believe it

sometimes would you believe it
he said to me
i chuck poems out at those editors
like bullets
or else
like rubbish
the dumping grounds

are everywhere in the world
for poetry
some poets are always gazing at their own shit
gathered there

that's all right
i said
as long as it proves they are alive

i wish i were dead
he said
rather than have to live with rubbish all my life

The stereotypical question

i really like stereotypes
(who doesn't?)
they are so easy to deal, and work, with
(malleable in fiction and poetry, as i said in my phd thesis)
to begin with
no one knows westerners better than a chinese
they (i mean westerners, not chinese)
have a big nose or hooked nose or eagle-hooked nose
they have sunken eyes or deep-seated eyes or big eyes
they are smelly in the armpits
they don't speak good chinese
(they don't even speak it)
old couples walk hand in hand on the streets
they (i mean young ones; i don't know about the old) like sex
they do it like sports
they have aids
they die of much happiness
fashioned out of advanced drug and technology
surfeited with sex
gluttons
and it's true
these are all malleable and easy stereotypes
that most chinese (like you and me) are comfortable with

now let me come to my point
how am i going to turn this western woman in my fiction
into something slightly more than a stereotype
that's different from you and me?

how am i going to turn
the stereotype into her
that is?

Statue of liberty

wondering

where

her

PEN IS

T

Talking with the famous writer

it's kind of funny you know
when i came back on the plane
i felt as if i was still with you
although we had had so much time talking to each other
mostly you about yourself
because you had so much to talk about
your y/ears were invincible
impervious to my intimacies
of an unknown life
thus i was left with the only choice of talking to myself as if
to you
your shadow in the dark recesses of the mind
i noticed that you were very clean a clean man in his early sixties
girls liked to have photos taken with you
something i resented
i came to understand that fame was a thing that could be
stolen easily by camera
you never asked anything about me
a sign that showed your egocentrism or nonchalance?
but you had to listen to me when i started talking about the
difficulty with
old writers in producing anything original anything even new
the early death of creativity
you kept silent and then went to bed unusually early
i knew i hurt you
so what
i'd never become famous as you
and never wanted to
didn't you realise the price you had to pay for such bloody fame
you were dragged around from place to place just to see things

like a tourist
you couldn't help criticise others more and praise yourself less
you probably did not like the way i did to you
by not joining the photograph crowd
you probably wondered why you should have come to such a point that you
had to put up with the people you would have ignored in sheer contempt
otherwise
such was fame that one was made less famable by a much-worn name
don't you know that no one can speak for anyone any more
don't you know that there is nothing in the centre at all
don't you know that the only thing that matters is someone you have
at your side even if it is only a dog or a cat or a rat or an inflatable doll
someone that you'll know that is you that is part of you
as you are him
the world oh the world
what does it matter
so long as you can find someone you can talk to

you'll go in a few days
and you took a cold farewell from me
which hurt me very much
your eyes seemed to be saying that nothing did matter
i was only one of those millions of nonentities you had met
and will keep meeting in the world
who came to you of their own accord milling around you like ants

so they should leave you alone of their own free will
you were probably right
but did you know that i did not take people like you very
seriously either
because there were so many like you who'd fade into history
who were already becoming history even when they were alive
what's the point of living like a piece of history
well let me finish here because the winter is on
and i have to hurry back to my den of dis/content
and prepare for a weeping winter without a cause

byeeeeeee

Temporarily untitled

the news came that the poet died
he had killed his wife and hang himself on a tree outside the house

on an island not far from auckland
called something i can't remember at all

because it is difficult to pronounce
the poet was really doing well

being a resident poet in a german university
and a new zealand university

he must have earned a lot of new zealand and german money
no doubt about it

but his poems came back to me
poems which i did not particularly like

being the sort of person who detests any poets with a fame
and famous poems i hate that kind of thing

the poems about his being inhabiting two worlds simultaneously
seeing this world from the other world

as if he was standing on the other side of the shore
the poems about nothing at all

is this what his poems are really about
or is it only my rewriting from a bad memory

but i do remember two things that he says
something like this:

*dark nights give me a pair of dark eyes
with which i search for bright light*

or this:

*words are like paper currency
so dirtied and worn in circulation*

– i could not somehow fall into sleep
was it because my wife did not come to my side in the separated quilt

or was it because of the image that disturbed my sleepy mind
that i saw a man coming out of the house with an axe dripping with blood

and walking towards a gum tree
gum tree? or whatever trees that are commonly found in new zealand

he walked towards it with a poetical step
he must be composing poems even when he was contemplating suicide

he must be thinking god this time no one could publish my poems
i mean no one could claim me possess me hold me

the air on the tiny island is so transparent that morning
that you can almost see through the sun

he does not even notice his wife's death convulsions
but makes a poetical noose and hangs himself

on a poe/tree
to shake off the shackles of the images of

an island and a man on a poe/tree
and a woman hacked dead by a poetical axe

i penetrated her in the next quilt
and saw darkness afterwards in the bright morning sun

Terminally poetic

can't help it
don't know how long it's going to last
how far it's going to be
where it's going to lead
where it's going to end
what's going to happen
won't give it a shit
terminally
poetic
when the words reach here
they hit the wall
the great wall of china
and i was suddenly reminded
of the words i saw
on the wall:

terminally
chinese

what does that mean?
i ask myself in dream
terminally poetic?
or
poetically terminal?
i can't remember
if there's a doctor
whether the doctor can cure
and whether the man terminally poetic
is not terminally ill

the upshot of it all is
i've arrived at this poetic terminal

The thing is

we laugh

when
someone

farts

Theory

have you got a theory?

when you started preparing for your phd
that's what your supervisor asked you

sometimes i find it similar to someone asking before you get married,
have you got a dick?

now i get dirty
and i should say sorry

millions of people have died
as a result of marxist theory in china

and a huge number of academics are turned into slaves
by derrida and the french theorists

and of course they have become professors, too
a bonus i guess

enslaving their imitators
getting credits in the refereed journal

theory
you son of a bitch

(refer back to stanza 4, please)

this is a pretty unhappy country

this is a pretty unhappy country
the busy become busier
the poor, poorer
and fatter
and quieter

looking from a distance
especially from a high rise in the city
it is a pretty
country

on closer inspection
there is shit
in everyone's smile
and eyes
even the beer
can't wash it clean

there's money for sure
and the mortgage
that keeps the poor poorer
and more invisible
and the rich
are dying an early death
of having too much money

and this we had called
a paradise
before we came
this shit
this shithouse
this shithole that looks so pretty
for the less merrys

This is not a dream

I point my remote control
at the city
and turn on
the underbelly

pressing 4
I wake up the dead
and watch
their beautiful stories

pressing 14
I see Melbourne drugged and drunk
flattened kissing a tree
livable as far as Kingsbury is concerned

pressing 18
you turn Casino into your home
and your self
an Australian dream

pressing my eyes the double zero
you end up with
this remote control
it's all yours

This poem has been revised at least three times

I was writing this poem I mean I was writing this poem in english
no I mean I was writing this poem in English
about the possibility of revision but I wasn't able to write it
and I ended up with something that I wasn't able to revise
no I was saying that I ended up with something that I was not able
to revise no I mean I was not able to write something better than what I had intended to
but actually I did intend to write something that I was not going to revise
I mean I did intend to write something in its first draft
no actually it is better to revise and have multiple drafts because it conforms
and confirms our view that writing is a mechanical process
I mean a mechanical process my spelling is poor
I beg your pardon our culture is superior because it is revised to whiteness
by deleting all the unwanted colours
yellow contains a low
black contains a lack
I am only repeating myself from a novel I wrote a few years ago that remains unpublished
'cause it needs revision as a white woman suggests
a white woman is so beautiful so white so revised
I want to fall in love with her or in Chinese climb up love with her
oh white woman you don't find me containing a low and a lack because I can't revise?
but I'm telling ya I have revised this one for at least three times

This poem has not been revised

I thought of this great writer whose constant advise is:
revise revise revise
I thought of this Chinese proverb that says:
(should I say 'that goes'?)
wen bu yan bai gai
What does it mean?
You mean what it means?
I thought of this editor who decided not to take on a manuscript
because it gave him the impression that it's presented in its first draft
I thought of this woman on television who did give me the impression
that she's presented in her fifth or sixth draft
I thought of a Christmas card that has a picture in it
that shows a beautiful coil of shit wrapped inside something
very shinily expensive
I thought of the slogan in my *yang* days:
Down with the Soviet revisionism!
I thought of my own devised slogan in my middle-aged days:
Down with the Australian revisionism!
I thought of so many breast revising themselves throughout
the world
at the time of writing
I thought *yang* should be 'young' and 'breast' should be 'breasts'
and 'advise' should be 'advice'
I thought of the Chinese proverb again:
an article does not tire of being revised a hundred times
I thought of the great writer and the small editor clapping
their hands
and I thought of the slogan:
Down with the Australian revisionism!

to a white/coloured editor

to a white/coloured editor
whose power lies in writing to me and saying
among other things meaning rejection of course
please enclose an ssae or irc
for the return of your fiction or poetry
I say
as I said before
and I say here again
accept it or trash it
why bother sending it back
at your expense
or mine
if you don't want to show
your 19th century power of rejection
with 21st century neo-colonialism
or else
let me bomb you with my blood
and see if you can reject it or accept it!

To all the poets i have read

yes I know your stuff
and what you'll say:

poetry should not mean
but be

be what?*
and poetry comes out of anger
or love or frustration or loneliness or sadness or war or
violence or hatred*
all the colours of feelingbow

now you can jaw!

for me
poetry is a laxative
I take to the toilet

if my bowels happen to be moved
i'm a happyman*

* 'B' in Chinese pronunciation sounds exactly the same as vagina – this poet's note.
* According to Chinese saying, a poet is a hating person – this poet's note.
* No, I can't…
(Sorry, the poet feels bad about having to explain too much to the five-year-old western reader who has so little knowledge of chinese.)
('the-five-year' is a reference to Martin Amis's comment on *Wild Swans* by Jung Chang as a book that makes him 'feel like a five-year-old'. *Wild Swans*, Flamingo, 1991)

to get an australian

to get an australian
citizenship
takes you about
2 yrs
of unbroken
stay
in australia
after you acquire
your permanent
residence

but to get
an australian
literary or poetic
citizenship
(such as that ordained by an oxford or a cambridge or a
literary red neck)
it takes god knows how long

longer
i'd say
than a poetic licence
certainly much longer
than an asian

To mankind

as long as you still eat meat
sheep/fish/pigs/bulls/birds/rabbits

wholesale or
retail

this tendency is still in you
to eat humans whole

one day when you run out of meat
to eat

To the age of unreason

the critic says:
oh he is a good poet
because he is so difficult

what he does not understand himself is that
he doesn't even understand himself
when he writes the poem

the poet or the writer or anyone with a pen in hand
or a computer in front of him for that matter
does not need his head to think
instead
a pig's head a dog's head a cow head a maiden head
an artificial head
anything but a human head
will do

it is fashionable to unthink
in an age of unreason
and good luck goodfuck to all the unreasonable critics
who are clever enough to work out the reason behind it all

To think

that up to this point billions of people have died
for money and money alone

it is perhaps not inapt to quote
the ancient chinese saying:

*man dies for money
as birds die for food*

while i'm still wondering
where my next cent comes from

To you in the bar

who stays
not the poets
who are going and gone
when the poetry is done

it's you
the drinking and drunk
who stay
and are staying
and will stay
for ton(gue)s of wine and y/ears of patience

so to you
i dedicate this bloody english po(e)m

U

Untitled

amidst life
there is death

as amidst peace
there is disturbance

amidst happiness
there is sadness

amidst comedy
there is tragedy

and amidst writing
there is the impulse

to unwrite

and amidst poetry-making
there is the constant desire

to unmake poetry

Untitled (b)

living in oblivion
like an australian
in between

continents
on the edge
of nowhere

living an oblivion
that no body cares
leaving to posterity

what is being
lived
and written

in oblivion

V

Vision

an australian poet friend wrote me today
rejecting an article of mine
and he used the word
which was responsible for this poem
the ideas for it I put down earlier in the day
in my car on a yellow sticker in the form of a few broken lines
but that is irrelevant
I wrote:

I don't have a vision
although i do have a tele
vision
in fact
I never have one
actually I hate the word
the simple reason I started a magazine
is because I now have the power of rejection
to be able to reject the famous names
if their stuff is not good enough
for my money
there are other reasons too
but this is the main one
as for the reason why I write
and write poetry in particular
I think it is simple
I mean writing poetry is simple for me

I write three or four a day on the average
and the one that won a prize
I produced in the matter of minutes
without the kind of revision that a novelist would always
insist on
I hate a novelist drudgery
with its mercenary connotations
and I write poetry
possibly because I can't do anything else
but that is not the main reason

although I now write novels myself
and don't mind revision, actually

W

Watching betty blue

typing her novel on the typewriter
and her man commenting on her beauty
which i see only in profile
and afterwards
in a bed after making love
i find everything so different from any american films
i've ever seen
that i hate american films
i hate them because they are like kentucky chicken
mass-produced
and tasteless

although i've seen it once
i'd like to see it again
but i have to get back to my novel
that i'm spending this Sunday to write
i, too

want to make it different
and un-american

What did they say when they read your poems

oh, that's a lovely poem
fantastic!
you wrote wonderful stuff!

I really enjoyed your poems
good, they are very good
excellent

I don't really know what to say
except:

thank you
thank you very much
thank you all

and wonder to myself:
why did I not hear one single bad comment?
but I did not have the heart to ask those who did not say a word
or perhaps they've already said it in their silence?

What is happening at this time of my life

I know the editors will say
I won't read this kind of mundane stuff again

fine with me

what is happening now is that the twentieth century
is fast dying, having spent its first five months and 12 days

and I am not having any sex with anybody, not even with myself
for a long time even though this world is now highly sex- charged

apart from making money and making poetry and making my
way out
I am not talking to anybody, either

or if I do
I am only talking to people of my own race

I now have the habit of wiping my mouth with my hands
from time to time, particularly the corners of my mouth

if someone happens to shake my hand at this juncture
he will get stained

I am washing my mouth with a kind of brown liquid daily
and it works wonders: blood no longer accompanies each
session of my teeth-brushing

there are other secret things that I enjoy doing
that other poets will employ metaphors similes figures of speech
to describe

but I have deliberately abandoned them
'cause all I need right at this moment

is to have someone to talk to
without resorting to rhetorical devices

knowing that it is 11.50 at night
with another day gone from the twentieth century, never to return

What's wrong?

love ends in
disasters

progress leads
nowhere

poetry prose prawn
third time lucky

writing is
heavy

making love is too
easy

20 and 21
only one more digit

What title do you think this should be?

paper printed
on
both sides
is
a frugal
way
with my solicitors
and barristers

do they realise
that in doing so
they are being
brutal
with their life
printed
on both

sides?

What went through my mind when I was looking at these empty slabs of bottles was that

if our magazine
literary

could sell

like these cans of coke cola
commercial

what I meant was that

if our mag.

could sell

like coke

would you believe i'm still a poet?

Who's to blame?

when the chinese go overseas and take to learn other languages
                                                                         and become others
who's to blame, themselves or others?

when china westernises itself by getting rid of all the cultural
                                                                         traditions it calls rubbish
who's to blame, china or the west?

when my son loses his chinese when my wife no longer wants
                                                                        to go back to china
who's to blame, my son or my wife?

when chinese women only want to marry the white men
who's to blame, them or the whites?

when all the non-western countries are turning westward
who's to blame, them or us?

when we are daily losing our mono-culture against the onslaught
                                                                             of many
who's to blame, ouyang yu or les murray?

when this poem is judged unpublishable
who's to blame, the poet or the editor?

why do we need to

why do we need to
be known to so
many people
+call it being well-known
let's work this out
a bit
suppose it's a pig
does a pig want to
be well-known
i suppose it doesn't
why should he
his meat being enjoyed by many
is not a pleasant business
in fact
it's cruel
to be fried stewed roasted + salted
aren't there times
when we may be friedstewedroastedsalted
like diana/clinton/you name it
why do you get upset
if your name is not included
along with other names
what's in a name
what's not in a name
are we born for it
do we die for it

because we don't want to be a pig?

Why do we so worry about the dates?

should I date it 22/09/00
and when it reaches midnight
should I date it 22nd or 23rd
what if my watch goes too slow or too fast
and it is daylight saving
what if the recorded date gets deleted because of an error in
the computer
does it matter if something I wrote is dated ten years ago
does that date it
or what if I delete the date
does that make it dateless and subsequently timeless
why are we so afraid of losing the dates for each particular
thing we write
are we too concerned for our after-life
do we think too far ahead
do we like to think someone whom we shall never know
but who will know us somehow through our poetry
in a couple of hundred years
will pick us up and put us in an anthology or something and
put a date to it
still, does that matter?
can they backdate it and what if they can
what if they can date it back to this very minute when I am writing
what does it matter if I update something I wrote many years ago
and backdate something I've just finished writing
why do we worry so much about dates?
we
of all the people
why do we treat dates as importantly as poetry itself
if not more
why date dates that date anyway?

why do we write

why do we write
i mean why do we write at all
it's not part of human nature to write isn't it
i mean who's reading you anyway these days
i mean you get published in some magazines
that can't even survive on their own
without the government's support
and then when they get published they'd find it hard to sell them
people who do appear in them only read themselves
like yourself isn't that right
but why do we write
i mean you don't even know who you write for these days
if you write in chinese by the time your stuff gets published
it's some thousand miles away in the mainland or taipei or singapore city
years later and who knows what you are talking about anyway
if you do that in english the chances are that your name may get into the bibliography
in the auslit. slightly better than chinese isn't it
still why write if you are not feeling sick
if you are not intent on getting some prizes maybe miles franklin
i'm sure few chinese or taiwanese or hong kongese have heard of this funny thing
nor do they really care like they do with nobel prizes
but why do you write and get published in things that few bother to read
and you never have any response to anything you write
a hopeless career
that you are stuck in

still want to convince yourself that you are a 'soul-engineer'
of people
or a soul-destroyer?
a writer
you have to live with this disease commonly called writing

in english it is writing/riting/righting
and in chinese it is *xie* (writing)/*xie* (letting out)/*xie* (releasing)/*xie* (discharging)

A word with the feminists

    yes
we'll fight
if you want to resort to
    violence
we'll resort to it
if you want theorising
    theorising it is
we'll even make
    love
if that's what you want
    your way
    for sure
come what may
until we die fighting
    or loving
embraced in our
    dead arms

World politics

the world is a two-party system
with the west currently in power
having voted itself in
and the east notwithstanding its power
sticking to the wilderness
until such a day comes
as the chinese saying goes:

30 years the river runs west
30 years the river runs east

any attempt to form a single party
is against the very idea of western democracy
and the very idea of eastern folk philosophy
about the renegade river that runs east and west
in a matter of decades
whether you dis/like it

Written at midnight

most books are beautifully
boring
when published
despite the
blurb
the
gloss
the
promotion
the pretty
publicists

they are
very
beautiful
beautifully
boring

the more money
spent
on advertising
the
more
boring
beautifully

Written by one who doesn't know how to write poetry

around 8.30 p.m., 15/05/00

i wish
i could
make my poems
as simple
and
straightforward
as rain
drops

immediately after this, 15/05/00

perhaps
it's not
a
bad idea
to
be buried
in
your own
car
like
a
coffin
as an american
painter did
in
a
t.v. show

9.51 p.m., 15/05/00

no
poetry works
for
the rich
as long and far as
the money
does

www.ingramcontent.com/pod-product-compliance
Lightning Source LLC
Chambersburg PA
CBHW071845080526
44589CB00012B/1115